ARTHUR KOE

MAKERS OF MODERN THOUGHT

EDITOR:

THE REV. DR. A. D. GALLOWAY

PROFESSOR OF DIVINITY, UNIVERSITY OF GLASGOW

CONSULTANT EDITORS: The Rev. Joseph D. Ban (Chaplain, Linfield College, McMinnville, Oregon, U.S.A.), the Rev. Alec Gilmore (Associate Editor, Lutterworth Press) and the Rev. Frank Hoadley (Editor, Judson Press, U.S.A.)

ARTHUR KOESTLER

by

WOLFE MAYS

LUTTERWORTH PRESS

GUILDFORD AND LONDON

First published 1973

by the Lutterworth Press, Luke House, Guildford, Surrey

American edition published by the Judson Press, Valley Forge, Pennsylvania

ISBN 0 7188 1918 7

Printed in Great Britain
at the St Ann's Press, Park Road, Altrincham, Cheshire,
WA14 5QQ

CONTENTS

INTRODUCTION

WHY is Arthur Koestler to be regarded as a maker of modern thought? He is neither a professional scientist who has made a profound discovery about nature or developed a theory which has changed our outlook upon it, nor a professional philosopher who has constructed a new system of ideas. He has not started or led a political movement, or set an example to the world by his moral stance. Nevertheless, his work is of importance on a number of counts. He was one of the first to show, through his political essays and novels, the dilemma of the modern intellectual who, on the one hand, is subject to the suffocating pressure of a totalitarian regime or the doctrinaire dictates of a political party, and, on the other, cannot but listen to his conscience which urges on him a more enlightened moral and political attitude, one in which the freedom of the individual is paramount.

His own political history exemplifies this internal struggle. He joined the Communist Party in his youth, only to be disillusioned and leave it. The Utopia he had hoped for had not come. He also had before him the poignant and tragic example of Germany where appeals to the more instinctive and emotional aspects of human nature—the twilight zone of men's minds—had brought about the Nazi regime and its aftermath of war, terror and extermination camps. He therefore argued that, in order to understand and change our political attitudes, we need to bring these unconscious drives out into the open, and see that they are used for more constructive purposes.

If Koestler's work had stopped at this point, he would perhaps have been seen as no more than a literary figure, depicting in his essays and novels the stresses and strains affecting political man—someone who had alerted us to the dangers inherent in the contemporary human predicament. But Koestler's original contribution, which gives him a place in this series, was to generalize and systematize this perception in the field of political behaviour and to show that the same instinctive and emotional drives were also at work in both the sciences and the arts. For example, he argued that scientists—especially great scientists—worked by hunches and intuitions and were often as dependent on happy accident for their discoveries as on cold logic. Koestler therefore believed that there were not really two cultures as, for example, C. P. Snow has argued. Political institutions, art, literature, drama, music, as well as natural science and mathematics, were all human products, which exhibited in various forms not only similar rational but also similar irrational tendencies.

In his emphasis on the more irrational aspects of human experience, Koestler has much in common with modern existentialist philosophers, but, unlike the latter, he does not neglect science. Because of this, he is acutely aware that man cannot find salvation in science alone, and in its values of neutrality, rationality and efficiency. After the atom bomb and Hiroshima, he is more than ever conscious of the need to develop the moral side of our natures if we are to continue living on this planet without destroying ourselves. Though Koestler does not accept a religious creed, he does indicate the need for a new faith if there is to be any hope for the future of mankind: spiritual values will have to replace the more material ones of our present culture.

1

LIFE

ARTHUR KOESTLER was born in Budapest on September 5, 1905, the only son of Henrik and Adela Koestler. He spent his early years in Budapest and Vienna, studied engineering at the *Technische Hochschule* in Vienna, and was a member of a duelling fraternity at the university there. He left in 1925, before completing his degree, to go to Palestine, where he spent some time in a communal settlement. Subsequently he became editor of a weekly paper in Cairo and then moved to Paris where he worked for the Ullstein News Service. In 1930 he transferred to Berlin to become science editor of the *Vossische Zeitung*. In 1931, he also became foreign editor of the *BZ am Mittag*, and took part in the *Graf Zeppelin* Arctic Expedition to the North Pole.

In 1931 occurred the event which he says was, after his birth, the most important in his life—he joined the Communist Party. He spent 1932-3 travelling in Russia and Soviet Central Asia. Koestler went to stay in Paris in 1934 when resistance to Hitler in Germany had been driven underground, and in 1936 during the Spanish Civil War he visited Spain as a journalist. In 1937 he visited Spain again and was arrested by Franco's Forces in Malaga. He spent three months in prison in Seville under sentence of death, but was released. *Dialogue with Death* (1940) is an account of his prison experiences.

When the Second World War broke out in 1939, he was in France and was sent to an internment camp at Le Vernet as a suspect alien. He later served in the French Foreign Legion, 1939-40. His book, *Scum of the Earth* (1941), deals with his experiences in Le Vernet. In 1940, Koestler escaped to England through Portugal, was imprisoned in Pentonville Prison and on his release served in the British Pioneer Corps, 1941-2.

Koestler has given us a very readable account of his life up to 1940, in his fascinating autobiography which appeared in two volumes. The first volume, *The Arrow in the Blue* (1952), dealing with the period 1905–1931, covers his childhood and youth until he became a member of the Communist Party—his student days, his stay in Palestine, and his experiences as a journalist in the Middle East, Paris and Berlin. The second volume, *The Invisible Writing* (1954), deals with the period 1932–1940—his early Communist days in Berlin and later in France, and covers his experiences in the Spanish Civil War and the early years of World War II. In these volumes Koestler makes some very frank disclosures about himself, especially his attitudes to sex and marriage, which give them something of the character of the classical confessions of St. Augustine and Rousseau. The reader may refer to them for further details of his active and colourful life. I shall content myself with such biographical detail as is necessary for tracing his development as a writer and a thinker, and showing that there is a certain basic pattern and continuity in his ideas.

In 1938 Koestler left the Communist Party, completely disillusioned with it and the Soviet leadership. His first novel, *The Gladiators* (1939), dates from this period. This work concerns the slave revolt led by Spartacus in Ancient Rome. It traces the failure of the revolution to deficiencies both in the leaders and the masses who at first followed them. Koestler sees it as an early example of a revolution which failed to achieve its objectives as a result of pressures from the masses who did not understand the 'law of detours' which their leaders found it necessary to employ, and which involved them in a conflict between ends and means.

In his most famous novel, *Darkness at Noon* (1940), the theme is once again a revolution which has failed—in this case the Russian Revolution. The book centres round the dilemma of an individual, a Commissar, who has to decide whether to continue supporting the party he has loyally served, or to follow his conscience and oppose its inhuman methods. The period covered is that of the thirties, when many of the leading Russian Communists who had helped to bring about the revolution were arrested and charged with crimes which they had not committed.

In many of Koestler's novels one sees a similar working out of an individual's personal conflicts in a stressful social or political situation. Thus in the novel, *Arrival and Departure* (1943), he is concerned with the psychological conflicts of a young refugee from Nazi oppression living in a neutral country, and he tries to analyse the unconscious motivations of revolutionary thought and action.

In *The Yogi and the Commissar* (1945), a series of essays on political questions, Koestler examines the various political attitudes found in modern society, and gives a critique of Soviet Communism. He discusses the question of ends and means, and condemns political action which makes the end subservient to the means. This work may be said to contain preliminary sketches of topics discussed in greater detail by Koestler in some of his later writings.

The dilemma between ends and means comes up again in the novel, *Thieves in the Night* (1946), although here it is given a different treatment. The novel is concerned with the Jews and their struggle in Palestine before the establishment of the State of Israel, and is no doubt partly based on Koestler's own experiences there. In it he gives a pragmatic defence of the use of violence in the struggle for the Zionist cause—the establishment of a Jewish National Home—which, at the time of Koestler's writing, was being frustrated by the Arabs and the then British administration. What Koestler seems to be saying is that there are situations in which violence is justifiable to achieve desirable ends. In *Promise and Fulfilment* (1949), a history of Zionism in Palestine covering the period 1917-49, Koestler puts forward similar arguments.

When Koestler turned to his earlier interests in science and psychology, he again attempted to bring about a synthesis between incompatible tendencies. This is particularly evident in *Insight and Outlook* (1949) and *The Act of Creation* (1964). In the former, he deals with the conflict between what he considers to be the two main springs of human conduct—the self-assertive and self-integrative (or self-transcending) ten-

11

dencies, as they show themselves in scientific discovery and artistic creation. Koestler hopes that he will thus be able to obtain an insight into the common foundations of science, art and social ethics. This theme is worked out in much greater detail and richness of example in *The Act of Creation*.

We have noted, particularly in the novels and political essays, Koestler's concern with the theme of the conflict of polar opposites, between which he attempts to achieve some sort of synthesis. It is therefore not surprising to find him saying that the drama and the novel thrive on conflict. The conflict, he tells us, may be fought out in the divided heart of a single character or between two or more persons or between a man and his destiny. All great literatures contain varieties and combinations of archetypal conflicts, examples of which are the death and rebirth *motif*, the strife between generations, and the taboo on incest.

In *The Sleepwalkers* (1959), which deals with Man's changing views about the universe, Koestler is critical of the view of religion as a mere superstition standing in the way of progress, and especially of the view that the advance of science is a rational, logical one. He argues that the great cosmological systems of Copernicus, Kepler, Brahe, Galileo and Newton reflect the unconscious prejudices, philosophical and political, of their originators. The manner in which some of the most important discoveries of science were made reminds one, Koestler says, more of a sleepwalker's performance than of a rational or logical advance. By thus enquiring into the workings of the creative mind and analysing the changing relations between scientific and religious insight, Koestler hopes to find a more unified system of thought.

During 1958-9, Koestler travelled to India and Japan and he reported on these travels in *The Lotus and the Robot* (1960), where 'Lotus' refers to agricultural India and 'Robot' to industrial Japan. Whilst in these countries he took a hard look at Yoga and Zen Buddhism. The East, he concludes, seems less interested in factual knowledge (*sophia*) of the external world, than in essential Being (*ousia*); it prefers intuition to reason, symbols to concepts, and self-realization through the unfolding of individuality to gain through conflict.

In *The Ghost in the Machine* (1967), Koestler returns to some of the questions dealt with in the more theoretical part of *The Act of Creation*, and develops his theory of hierarchical structures which he believes underlie all organic and social life. Koestler is here critical of the slot-machine behaviourist model of man based on the mechanistic world view of the nineteenth century. He does not think we shall be able to ask the right questions until we have a broader conception of human reality. He is hostile to any attempt to reduce man to the lower aspects of his animal nature, and to try to interpret his behaviour, as some psychologists have done, in terms of the rat. In *Beyond Reductionism* (1969), a symposium edited with J. C. Smythies, he continues to oppose certain reductionist theories in science.

Koestler takes up again his evolutionary interests in *The Case of the Midwife Toad* (1971), in which he concerns himself with the work of Dr. Paul Kammerer, a Viennese experimental biologist. Kammerer's work on the midwife toad is said to have provided evidence for the Lamarckian view of evolution, namely, that acquired characteristics are inherited. He committed suicide after his vital specimen had been shown to have been 'doctored'. In going over the evidence again, Koestler concludes that, since Kammerer's work had been bitterly attacked by the neo-Darwinians who upheld the theory of chance mutations preserved by natural selection, he may have been just as much a victim of unreason as were the more numerous past victims of political and religious persecution. Koestler shows some sympathy for the neo-Lamarckian position, since he believes that if the neo-Darwinians are right, evolution and human history become completely void of significance.

Koestler's latest non-fictional work is *The Roots of Coincidence* (1972). He is concerned here with such topics as extra-sensory perception, modern particle physics and the nature of coincidence.

13

2
THOUGHT
A. POLITICAL AND SOCIAL THINKING
Koestler's Disenchantment with Communism

KOESTLER, in common with many intellectuals in the late thirties, was particularly disappointed by the outcome of the Russian Revolution. They had high hopes that it might lead to a Utopia. This never materialized, and Soviet Russia developed a form of State Capitalism, while both internally and externally its politics took a pronounced nationalistic turn. Indeed, in 1944 the national anthem was changed from the 'International' to one extolling 'Russia the Great'[1]. After obtaining power, the leaders' aim seemed to be to retain it at any price, even if it meant, as it did, abandoning early ideals. A major theme of Koestler's political writings is the decadence of the Revolution owing to the corrupting effects of power. Orwell remarked, however, that Koestler had a somewhat optimistic view of human nature: 'perhaps the choice before man is always a choice of evils . . . All revolutions are failures, but they are not all the same failure'.[2]

Koestler was concerned with the way Communist Russia had treated its staunchest supporters, particularly the old Bolsheviks, who had suffered for the cause under the Tsarist regime and during the Revolution. In *Darkness at Noon* he ~es up this matter in some detail. The central character of the ~~ a Commissar, N. S. Rubishov, a faithful party member ~~ever, has in the past had twinges of doubt about the ~~ methods. He has been arrested on charges of ~~abotage, of which he is innocent. The narrative ~~ment, trial and execution, and gives occasional flashbacks to his revolutionary past. Rubishov at first denies and then ultimately confesses to crimes which he has never committed. Koestler says that this work is based on the real life indictment of such men as Bukharin. As he puts it, 'The characters in this book are fictitious. The historical circumstances which determined their actions are real. The life of the man N. S. Rubishov is a synthesis of the lives of a number of men who were victims of the so-called Moscow Trials'.[3]

According to Orwell, the whole book centres round the question, why did Rubishov confess?[4] The confessions obtained in the Russian State Trials are, he points out, capable of three explanations: (1) that the accused were guilty; (2) that they were tortured and perhaps blackmailed by threats to relatives and friends; (3) that they were actuated by despair, mental bankruptcy and the habit of loyalty to the Party. Koestler, he says, rules out (1) since the trials seem to have been a frame-up. Some of Koestler's critics who believed in the guilt of the accused, did not agree with this verdict on the proceedings. As Caute remarks, 'They confessed because they were caught red-handed and there was no way out'.[5] Orwell's second explanation is the common sense one. (3) is accepted by Koestler, since he believes Rubishov confessed because he could not find any reason for not doing so. Faced with having to decide between allegiance to the Party and confessing to non-existent crimes, he is unable to put his past devotion to the Party behind him, and he chooses to continue to serve it in the only way he now can, and is shot. Rubishov, Koestler argued, confessed out of self-sacrificing devotion to the Party.

The book, it is pointed out,[6] is not merely a study of Rubishov's attempt to reconcile his conscience with the dictates of the Party. It attempts to state a defence of the Party, and to explain why it had acted in the way it did in instigating the political purges. Starting from the Communist assumptions of the regime, it puts forward a set of consistent arguments justifying the terrorist methods used. In the discussions between Rubishov and his interrogators, these arguments are logically developed, and Rubishov is so struck by their cogency that he comes to see why it is necessary for him to continue supporting the Party and its actions.

A good deal of the contemporary interest of *Darkness at Noon* is now lost, but in a sense it still remains topical. The problem it discusses, the individual's freedom of speech and action within a restrictive political system, is still with us. It is perhaps most clearly seen today in the plight of the creative writer within a totalitarian state.

* * * *

Darkness at Noon had little impact when it was first published in Britain. On the other hand, when it appeared in France after the last war under the title *Le Zéro et l'Infini*, it immediately achieved a *succès de scandale*, and was denounced or praised largely in accordance with the political complexion of the critic. It led Maurice Merleau-Ponty, a distinguished French philosopher and a friend and colleague of Jean-Paul Sartre, to devote a book *Humanisme et Terreur*[7] to an analysis of Koestler's views, and to an attempt to justify the use of violence in Soviet Russia by Stalin and the Russian leaders.

Merleau-Ponty, a Marxist himself, though he later turned against Soviet Communism, was highly critical of Koestler's explanation of the confessions.[8] He points out that in Koestler's account Rubishov is deposed because he does not support the new political orientation of the Party, and since Rubishov's morality has always been to support the Party, he ends up by confessing. Merleau-Ponty contrasts this with the actual case of Bukharin, who, he says, remains a person. He defends his revolutionary honour and rejects the imputation of espionage and sabotage. When Bukharin capitulates, he recognizes in his political conduct an inevitable ambiguity.

Merleau-Ponty argues that the phenomenon of the self-accusations of the defendants must be understood from the point of view of what he calls the ambiguity of history. He explains this by saying that it is possible that a person will not realize the full meaning of his actions until a later date, so that at any particular time it is not clear whether the approved Party line really serves the interest of the proletariat. In such cases individuals may plot against the State and plan a revolt. But, Merleau-Ponty asks, do they know clearly and distinctly what they are doing? Only the course of history will show the

16

meaning, and consequently the morality, of their actions, but this will not be an absolute meaning. For it is always possible that the condemned may one day be rehabilitated, when a new phase of history has changed once more the meaning of their conduct.

Merleau-Ponty would seem to be arguing in favour of the guilt of the defendants, but he gives his argument a subtle twist: their actions, he says, were ambiguous. Although they may have thought at a particular time that what they were doing was right, at a later date they have come to realize that their actions were misguided. But he does not rule out the possibility that in the course of history circumstances may change and their actions be vindicated. Merleau-Ponty does seem to be acting as an apologist for the Soviet regime here, but his point is nevertheless a valid one. Evaluations of historical events and persons do change from period to period. For example, estimates of Napoleon have varied considerably over the years. After first being depicted in Britain as 'Boney'—a child-eating ogre—he came to be regarded as one of the great military geniuses of our time. For Merleau-Ponty there is no such thing as history apart from our interpretation of it. When Rubishov returns to his cell after confessing, he invents good reasons to justify the actions of the Party but, as Merleau-Ponty points out, it is Rubishov himself who interprets the historical situation. Hence, he argues, there is always in his view of the situation a risk of error and a chance of partiality, and the question still remains whether Rubishov has not rationalized his position so as to make his peace with the Party and because it is hard to be alone.

Merleau-Ponty believes that the inhuman dilemma in which Rubishov finds himself, whether to heed the voice of his conscience or to accept the dictates of the Party, arises because he accepts a mechanistic rather than a Marxist philosophy of history, namely, one which accepts the inevitableness of the course of history against which the individual is helpless. But, Merleau-Ponty goes on, Marx in his philosophy of history took account of the part played by consciousness in the achievement of the revolutionary process, so that the individual has a say in his destiny.

Merleau-Ponty contrasts this approach with that of Rubishov, and by implication with Koestler's outlook on history. Rubishov, he says, voices the belief that when in the distant future history has become a science, it will eliminate the subjective element in our appreciation of history. And as long as this is not achieved 'politics would remain blood-stained dilettantism, mere superstition and black magic'.[9] But, Merleau-Ponty again points out, this is not the Marxist conception of historical truth: for Marx there are only human points of view, however relative they be.

Koestler does indeed say, 'The most evident hypothesis at our present state of knowledge is that the movements of history are determined by laws of a statistical nature, analogous to the physical laws of probability'.[10] He explains this further by saying, 'A great mass of people exposed for a long time to certain forms of pressure—climatic, economic, etc.—will sooner or later react in certain roughly predictable ways'.[11] But he makes the point that there is a margin in which the subjective factors of chance and leadership can exert their influence, and that for a short stretch of time, of say a hundred or so years, these factors may make a considerable difference. But in the long run the importance of the subjective factor becomes negligible and statistical probabilities become certainties.

For Koestler, the human factor in history is then important, but for him it only seems to have a transitory influence on the overall drift of historical change. Yet, without entirely subscribing to the view that had Cleopatra's nose been a little shorter the whole destiny of Europe would have been different, one cannot overlook the part played by great men (and women) in history, whether they be Napoleons or Newtons. Such individuals and their works seem to have had a more long-term effect than the hundred or so years which Koestler allots to them. If history is purely a human enterprise, then the long-run certainties of a science of history conjured up by Koestler would be an example of what he has been warning us against: moving from a level of human experience, where the historian is concerned with tracing the feelings, wishes and thoughts of men as expressed through their actions, to a more abstract level where individuals become vital statistics, and are considered solely in terms of the laws of statistical probability.

According to Merleau-Ponty, Koestler is essentially concerned with a problem which he never really formulates: can revolution avoid terror?[12] Communism, Merleau-Ponty says, did not invent violence, it found it established. In nominally liberal regimes, it is camouflaged under the name of legal, police and military sanctions. The question, he says, is not whether one accepts or rejects violence, but whether the violence one engages in is 'progressive' and tends to abolish violence, or whether it perpetuates itself. To decide this, one has to place the 'crime' within its historical context instead of judging it abstractly.

Curiously enough, as we have seen, Koestler puts forward a somewhat similar argument to justify the use of violence during the so-called Jewish terror in Palestine.[13] However, this attempt to justify violence in terms of special circumstances, gives a relativity to values which could be used to justify almost anything. Merleau-Ponty himself recognizes that if we attempt to use violence to bring about a better society, the means may become separated from the end, and unlimited terror may result. Perhaps there still is a place for tolerance and good sense in our civilization, something which Koestler campaigns for in most of his writings.

* * * *

Koestler returned to the Moscow trials and the problems surrounding the confessions in *Drinkers of Infinity*. He refers to one critic's statement that he had conferred on them a 'sinister dignity' which they did not possess, namely, that the accused renounced their lives as a last service to the Party. If we are to believe Khrushchev, the critic went on, torture and the bait of peaceful dachas were the things that induced Stalin's victims to incriminate themselves. To this Koestler replies that he only said that *very few* confessed in order to do the Party a last service. He does not dispute that others may have confessed after torture. But, he goes on, 'the old Bolshevik guard, the Bukharins, the Zinovievs and Piatakovs, were great men, and it would be the final injustice to misinterpret the motives for which they died'.[14]

Koestler considers this question to be as important as ever, because it is reported that brainwashing is still going on in China. It was practised on captured American soldiers in the Korean war and is, he claims, a variant of the psychological technique used on the old Bolsheviks. But what is now called brainwashing does not seem very different from what in the past was called indoctrination. Both Marxists and Catholics have employed methods of indoctrination, yet they have been prepared to discuss their doctrines rationally, since they hold them to be indubitably true. Indeed, a feature of *Darkness at Noon*, is the rational discussion which goes on between Rubishov and his interrogators, who finally convince him that the only way he can continue to serve the Party is by confessing.

In *Drinkers of Infinity*, Koestler tried to answer John Strachey (a one-time Communist himself) who had criticized what he called the 'literature of the disenchantment', which he asserted was exemplified in Koestler's writings as well as in those of such authors as Orwell and Pasternak. According to Strachey, the values of *Darkness at Noon* were not only subversive of the values of present-day Communism, but were also a reaction against the five hundred years of rationalism and empiricism, namely, the Enlightenment. As he saw it, the book was 'the starting point of the literature of reaction . . . the retreat from rationalism'.[15]

To this Koestler replies that whether reason is taken in the everyday sense as the power of thinking in ordinary and sensible ways, or, as some philosophers do, as a kind of universal goodness, in neither case would it be true to say that the 'literature of the disenchantment' represents a retreat therefrom. What it does reject is nineteenth century mechanistic philosophy, utilitarianism, and especially the view that the end justifies the means. However, Koestler here seems to be confusing the private philosophy of Stalin and the Soviet leaders with that of Marxism, from which Soviet Communism seems to have diverged. Whatever one thinks of Marxism, it certainly cannot be identified with mechanical materialism nor with Benthamite Utilitarianism. The actions of the Soviet leadership, with their acceptance of the philosophy that the end justifies the means, seem little different from those of earlier tyrants in the history of mankind, whatever their political colour may have been.

Politics and Human Behaviour

In *The Yogi and the Commissar*, Koestler conceives of an instrument—a sociological spectroscope—which would enable us to break up patterns of social behaviour, much as a physicist breaks up a beam of light.[16] On the infra-red end of the rainbow-coloured spectrum we would, he says, see the Commissar who believes in change from without (i.e. through revolution), that the end justifies the means, in logical reasoning, and that the universe is a mechanical system. At the other end, the ultra-violet, we find the Yogi. The latter believes that the means are alone important, that change can only come from within, through contemplation: he rejects violence and distrusts logical reasoning. In between are to be found a number of more sedate attitudes, such as Quakerism, Liberalism and Fabian Socialism.

Koestler notes two reasons why attempts to change the nature of man by Commissar methods have failed.

First, in most revolutionary movements the Utopian ideals of the leadership have had to be modified as a result of pressure from the masses, who have been more concerned with the satisfaction of their immediate needs; so that the whole movement eventually comes to nothing. This is a point with which Koestler is much concerned in his novel, *The Gladiators*.

Secondly, either the means are subordinated to the ends or *vice versa*. In the former case, you may attempt to justify your actions by slogans, such as 'the right of self-defence' or 'the best defence is attack'. The latter method, which seems to be much more characteristic of Yogi inaction, is just as futile. Koestler quotes the example of Ghandi, who preached non-violence and in World War II advocated non-resistance to an imminent Japanese invasion of India.

The prospects for the masses, he concludes, are then no brighter under the Yogi than under the Commissar, and he finds no political salvation in either. What he thinks is needed is some adequate *rapprochement* between the two.

Koestler tells us that in contrast to the nineteenth century when there was both in philosophy and in science a move towards the infra-red end of the spectrum, there is now a movement in the other direction, a tendency particularly marked in present-day science and above all in physics. Physics is not only unable to explain adequately, but it is also unable to describe what exactly is going on in the physical world. As examples, he quotes the discontinuity of quanta, the statistical nature of physical laws and the fact that determinism only applies on the macroscopic level. To a certain extent, he says, this change in physics has affected the artist, and the revolution in psychology has in turn influenced politics. But such influences are, he recognizes, at the most indirect. There is, for example, no causal link between quantum mechanics and the self-accusations of Bukharin. Nevertheless, he believes they have something in common. This he describes as an 'anti-materialist nostalgia', which is 'allergic to the rationalism, the shallow optimism, the ruthless logic, the arrogant self-assurance, the Promethean attitude of the nineteenth century; it is attracted by mysticism, romanticism, the irrational ethical values, by mediaeval twilight'.[17] Koestler sees historical change as a series of such pendular movements from rationalistic to romantic periods.

Merleau-Ponty argues, however, that if Koestler rejects nineteenth century materialism, he ought not also to throw out, as it were, the baby with the bath water, namely the advances of the nineteenth century, and try to substitute for it an anti-materialist nostalgia which, Merleau-Ponty asserts, can be as little understood by the masses as was materialism itself.[18] He also challenges Koestler's statement that science has usurped the claim of the other mode of knowledge—contemplation—for three centuries. As counter examples he mentions the attempt of Descartes, the seventeenth century French philosopher, to base the truth of things on our indubitable awareness of our own existence (*cogito ergo sum*), and that of the German philosophers, Kant and Hegel, who tried to construct the world in terms of mental categories.[19] But

22

Koestler's point is rather that the art of contemplation which he is urging us to adopt is of the non-rational sort found, for example, in aesthetic experience, and as such is not necessarily based on our understanding.

By way of a general criticism, it might be argued that Koestler's disjunction between the Commissar, who is only concerned with the external world and causal explanation and who operates according to the laws of a cruel logic, and the Yogi who is taken up with the contemplative life, is a highly artificial one. It resembles Descartes' dichotomy of mind and body, which among other things leads to the conflict between freedom and determinism, a problem with which Koestler is much concerned. The 'Yogi' and the 'Commissar', as Koestler well recognizes, are not real individuals but symbolic types like the 'average man'. One might argue that instead of trying to synthesize these two ideal incompatible types—a futile task anyway—we ought rather to return to our original unsophisticated experience, in which the sharp distinction between 'objective' and 'subjective' is not yet made. Koestler comes close to this when he says that the mystic, the lover, the artist, strive to recapture on a higher level the primitive oceanic feeling of the child.[20]

* * * *

Koestler has made an interesting attempt to analyse political behaviour in terms of Sigmund Freud's psychoanalytical theory.[21] He believes that in our study of political behaviour we ought to look more closely at the individual. We shall then discover that his actions are motivated not merely by past historical and material factors, but also by psychological ones. The case histories of most revolutionaries reveal a neurotic relationship with family or society, and this may exhibit itself as a moral conflict.

In his essay, 'A Guide to Political Neuroses', Koestler suggests that twentieth century man is a political neurotic. This is especially so in the case of the intellectual who is subject to tension: he aims towards a pure Utopia and revolts against present-day society. As Koestler points out, hatred of the existing order does not necessarily produce the charity and justice on which a Utopian society must be based.[22] In attempting to change society the intellectual has not been very successful. This is because he has started from the belief in the basic political sanity and rationality of man. This belief has been implanted in us during the Age of Enlightenment, 'by a long succession of French, German, and English philosophers —by Encyclopaedists, Marxists, Benthamites, Owenites, and Progressives of all shades'.[23] Freud has, Koestler says, undermined the optimistic belief in the rationality of man in the realm of sex, but it has not been adequately recognized 'that our political libido is just as complex-ridden, repressed and twisted, if not even more'. [24]

Koestler compares the neurotic's distorted universe, in which no factors are admitted which may upset its inner consistency, to that of the political neurotic, who also has an inner censor which protects his illusions of reality. 'The political neurotic carries his private Iron Curtain inside his skull'.[25] And this, he says, is much more effective than any totalitarian censorship, as arguments cannot penetrate 'the buffers of casuistry, the semantic shock-absorbers, the emotional defences'.[26] Koestler believes that in the field of political behaviour most people do not outgrow their early emotive states, so that their reasons for supporting political parties are usually highly irrational. Just as in the case of the sexual libido, where the internal censor has repressed unpleasant facts into the unconscious, which follows rules different from those of the conscious mind, so the political unconscious exhibits its own logic, symptoms and symbols. Koestler illustrates this by giving examples of repressed complexes in the field of the political libido:—[27]

1. *Repressed guilt*. He quotes the somewhat muted reaction of well-meaning Germans, when one mentions to them the extermination centres of Auschwitz and Belsen, in which many millions of people were put to death during the closing phases of the last war.

2. *Collective amnesia*. Koestler says that shortly after the Anglo-American liberation of France in World War II, the average Frenchman became honestly convinced that

France had never been defeated and that she had been saved by her own efforts.

3. *Escape from reality*. Koestler refers to what he claims is a specific British vice—the denial of unpleasant facts, often hidden, he says, behind an appearance of sweet reasonableness.

Koestler lists a number of minor aberrations which have their counterpart in the psychopathology of everyday political life.:[28]

1. *Ambivalence*. In neurotic behaviour an emotion may be succeeded by its opposite, blind infatuation by blind hatred. Koestler points out that many ex-Communists, ex-Catholics and ex-patriates fall into this attitude of the disappointed lover towards the party, church or country which once meant everything to them. No doubt his own reactions to Communism might be interpreted in some such terms.

2. *Fetishism*. Here the sexual instinct becomes attached to ordinary objects, which then take on a sexual significance for the individual. In the political field, he says, the fetish character of such symbols as flags, uniforms, songs and anthems, is sufficiently obvious.

3. *Eternal adolescence*. Examples of this are to be found among some radical intellectuals, who never seem to grow up politically. They remain to the very end eternal adolescents.

4. *The desire to belong*. By this, Koestler has in mind the individual's urge to identify himself with an idea, a set of values embodied in a community; this, he assumes, parallels the sexual urge to perpetuate the race.

The parallels drawn between the repressed complexes and minor aberrations in the sexual libido and deformed behaviour in the political libido, are undoubtedly both interesting and significant. But there also seem to be important differences. For example, the *repressed guilt*, which he finds among well-meaning Germans when confronted with the facts about the extermination centres (if it is really guilt and not simply discomfort in the face of unpleasant facts), may be a more conscious form of concealment than is the case with the Freudian Oedipus Complex (the desire to marry one's mother and to kill one's father). Or consider his concept of *collective amnesia*. This seems as dubious a concept as 'collective guilt'. It may be that some, or even most, Frenchmen behave in this

25

way, but it still does not follow that it is a syndrome due to completely unconscious factors. In the case of the typically British vice of *escape from reality* by ignoring unpleasant facts, the sweet reasonableness noted by Koestler may involve a conscious effort to be nice to others. These deformations of the political libido seem to be examples of self-deception, what Jean-Paul Sartre has called bad faith, rather than manifestations of repressed complexes. As for the minor aberrations of political behaviour, the analogy is here perhaps more precise.

* * * *

Koestler does not doubt that reason may and ought to be an ultimate criterion of our political ideals. Nevertheless, he believes that the Socialist movement has had too great an admiration for reason, and that this was why it foundered in Germany during the Nazi period. It did not appeal—as did Nazism—to the more mystical aspects of human experience, which religion normally takes account of. The Nazi movement succeeded because it had a greater emotional attraction for the masses. As an example of this, one may refer to the Nuremberg rallies, with their dramatic appeal to the more tribal instincts of the German *Volk*: the torch-light processions, marching men, and martial music. And Hitler himself was depicted in the popular imagination as a knight errant combating the wicked dragons of Communism and International Jewry.

One of the attractions of Marxism has been that it gives a consistent account of the normal behaviour of men and so provides a basis for a theory of political conduct. It appeals to the presumed fact that most people are primarily concerned with their own material or economic interest. Koestler does not, however, deny the importance of economic factors and social pressures in the determination of political behaviour. No psychiatrist can cure poverty and disease among the vast populations of Asia, he says. But he goes on to note that the crucial point is that before the economic needs of people express themselves in political action, a mental process intervenes which may initiate action directly opposed to the need. Thus, 'even highly civilized people like the Germans are capable of committing collective suicide, driven by some neurotic obsession and regardless of economic reality'.[29] Hence, in our analysis of political behaviour, we need to take account of psychological factors as well as economic ones.

Although Koestler demonstrates that the psychological dimension is important for our understanding of political behaviour, he does not make clear whether the political libido is reducible to the sexual libido, or whether he is simply using this concept to show that significant similarities are to be found between sexual behaviour and political behaviour. From what Koestler has said about the dangers of reducibility in ethics, he ought to be hostile to any attempt to reduce political values to elements belonging to a lower, more instinctive level. Political values themselves as normative ideals are, of course, never adequately achieved in actual political conduct, where not only one may act contrary to one's self-interest but also contrary to what a reasonable and just person would do.

On the other hand, the inconsistencies Koestler finds in the behaviour of politicians are not necessarily a sign of irrational factors at work, but may be due to the Machiavellianism of the political process itself. It could be argued[30] that the politician is not exhibiting emotional instability when, for example, he supports a policy in public of which he privately disapproves, but is coolly and rationally accepting a lesser evil. Still, this does not entirely get over Koestler's criticism that the politician may make his decisions irrationally, and then give a rational explanation for them, believing that he is coolly weighing up alternatives when all the time he has acted in accordance with his inbuilt prejudices.

Instinct and Emotion

Koestler tells us that the two basic drives underlying all our conduct are the self-transcending and self-assertive tendencies. What the self-transcending emotions have in common, according to him, is the feeling of integrative participation with others i.e., sympathy or identification. Examples of such emotions are joy, sadness, tenderness and compassion. Koestler is critical of their neglect by contemporary psychology. This, he believes, is due to the fact that these emotions, unlike the self-assertive ones, do not give rise to observable muscular activity, but to quietude, grief or aesthetic pleasure. Such emotive states as laughter and tears, awe and wonder, religious and aesthetic feeling—'the whole "violet" side of the rainbow of emotions'— have, he says, been left to the poets to worry about.[31] Although Koestler's remarks have some substance, the study of what might be termed the tender emotions has not been entirely neglected by psychologists. In the psychology of religion one may quote among others, William James' *Varieties of Religious Experience*.[32] Similarly, in the field of moral judgment, there is Jean Piaget's classic *Moral Judgment in the Child*. Psychologists have over the years also concerned themselves with the nature of aesthetic judgment.

Koestler explains why the self-transcending (integrative) emotions have been neglected in present-day civilization.[33] Social conditions during and after the Industrial Revolution increasingly discouraged contemplation, emphasis being put on self-assertive activities—domination, competition and individualism. In the East, on the other hand, the integrative tendencies of non-attachment, passivity and contempt for the body were encouraged. To overcome the hypertrophy of the self-assertive drives which Koestler believes to be at the root of the present-day ills of our civilization, he argues that not only do we need social and political reforms, but we also need to strengthen the self-transcending impulses. But he does not believe that a return to religion or pure mysticism will help us here. What we need, he says, is a new spiritual revolution.

Koestler links up his account of the polarity (or opposition) of the self-assertive and integrative tendencies with the view that the elements of living organisms have the dual attribute of partness and wholeness (or are Janus faced). He considers the two tendencies to be examples of this duality. Each organism, or its component parts, acts as an autonomous self-governing whole on its subordinate parts on lower levels of an organic or social hierarchy. By a hierarchy, Koestler has in mind here a special type of organization in which overall control is centralized at the apex, as in a genealogical tree which branches downwards.[34] One example of this would be a military hierarchy, where orders are directed downwards from the commanding officer through his subordinate officers to the lower ranks. On the upper limit of the organic hierarchy we find the same double aspect; the individual animal or man is a whole relative to part of his body, but a part relative to the social organization to which he belongs. All the more social forms of organization, Koestler states, are hierarchies. Thus not only would a human being or an animal be such a hierarchy involving different levels of organization, but so also would be the family and other social groupings.

Koestler maintains that the polarity between the integrative and self-transcending impulses applies throughout the organic realm. He believes this principle has a wider range of application than Freud's pair of instinctive drives:[35] *Eros* (the pleasure principle) and *thanatos* (the death instinct). On Freud's theory, he says, the ego's relations to other persons can only be either sexual or destructive. The more altruistic notions, such as comradeship, devotion to an ideal, are all regarded as sublimated forms of infantile sexuality. This leaves no place for any positive values in the field of ethics or social behaviour. For Freud, then, civilization leads to frustration and neurosis, driving underground these primitive urges, which avenge themselves by producing pathological phenomena. Koestler, however, rejects this somewhat jaundiced view of civilization. He believes that specific disturbances, such as revolutions arising in any given period and culture, are rather the result of faulty integrations of the social whole, and are to be looked upon as attempts by society to reach a stable state of equilibrium.

Koestler objects to Freudian theory on three counts:

1. He denies the instinctive character of aggressive or destructive behaviour (i.e., the death instinct), which he takes to be a form of self-assertion under conditions of extreme stress.

2. He asserts the integrative tendency to be genetically prior to the sex drive (pleasure principle); for Koestler the latter is merely one of the many integrative forces in animal and human societies.

3. He denies Freud's view that our instinctive drives tend to regress to lower levels of behaviour. The process of subli-

mation and inhibition of such drives, which for Freud forms the basis of civilization and give it its pathological character, are for Koestler a further development of biological and social evolution. If Koestler's position were consistently worked out in the field of political behaviour, the repressed complexes he discerns in the working of the political libido would then require expression in terms of a conflict between the self-assertive and self-transcending impulses.

These two principles or emotive attitudes postulated by Koestler seem to be blanket expressions covering a variety of different phenomena. The integrative tendency occurs in 'get together' situations and the self-assertive tendency in 'get out of here' situations. But if the features of these instinctive drives are dependent on the situation in which they occur, are we justified in assuming that they are processes or forces within the organism itself? Koestler himself has tried to explain Freud's death instinct by saying that it is a variation of the self-assertive instinct in situations of extreme stress. But could one not also say the same thing about the self-assertive drive—that it occurs only in challenging situations, and is hence a variation of some other more generalized instinct?

To summarize: for Koestler, not only are these two principles found in human society, but they also occur in the most primitive forms of life. On this level, he identifies them with the integrative and differentiating tendencies of living organisms —with their whole and part relationships. At a higher level, as we have seen, Koestler believes that these tendencies roughly correspond to Freud's pleasure principle and death instinct, but he regards them to be genetically more primitive than the Freudian ones. However, these broad descriptive categories are applicable to each evolutionary level in the biological hierarchy, and so Koestler does seem to overlook the important question, which is: what are the specific processes which at each level bring about such integration and differentiation?

It might therefore be argued that the similarities Koestler sees between (a) the self-transcending and self-assertive tendencies which occur in varying forms in human and animal behaviour, (b) the integrative and differentiating tendencies in the biological field, as seen, for example, in cells which fuse with one another and divide into smaller parts; and (c) the general concept of whole and part, are not as significant as he assumes. Perhaps it is a little remiss of him to assume that because such broad resemblances occur, they are manifestations of a single principle in nature. The most he can demonstrate is that at all levels in the organic and social hierarchies, whole and part relationships may be found. But this throws no light at all on the different qualitative features these whole and part relationships possess.

Freedom, Values and Reductionism

The problem of free-will and determinism is one which has occupied Koestler since his student days. He relates in his autobiography how in Vienna after a spirited discussion with another student on the problem of freedom versus determinism, he burnt his Matriculation Book (no doubt to show he was a free agent) and thereby put an end to his potential career as an engineer. He puts the dilemma posed by this problem as follows: according to science, man is no more free in the choice of his actions than a robot, but he cannot help believing he is free and personally responsible for his actions. On the psychological plane, he points out, the experience of freedom is as much a given fact of experience as are sense-perception and the feeling of pain.

Koestler tries to give ethics and aesthetics some sort of natural foundation, by giving values a place within his hierarchical theory of different levels of organization.[36] On this theory, laws of a higher level cannot be reduced to or predicted from those of a lower level, although lower level phenomena and their laws are implicit in the higher order. In aesthetics, ethics and the theory of knowledge, he goes on, much confusion arises because we apply specific laws of one level of reality to another, as when we attempt to reduce ethical values to biological or psychological concepts.

In his discussion of aesthetic values, Koestler quotes Freud's essay on 'A Childhood Memory of Leonardo da Vinci', in which Freud gives an analysis of the Mona Lisa in terms of

Leonardo's youthful development. Koestler says that although this analysis is of considerable interest as a piece of applied psychology, it explains nothing about the aesthetic value of the portrait—something which Freud recognized. Koestler argues that the so-called better understanding of an artist's work gained by reading his biography, or by historical introduction to his work, is a reductive understanding which interferes with our appreciation of aesthetic values. He comments that ever since he read Freud's 'Leonardo', 'I can't help seeing the Gioconda as a pathological exhibit'.[37]

What does seem rather odd is that in the field of science Koestler is doing very much the same sort of thing as Freud was in the realm of art. For example, in *The Sleepwalkers*, which was, of course, written at a later date, Koestler discusses with some relish and also good purpose the private lives of Copernicus, Galileo, Kepler and Newton in connection with their contributions to scientific thought. It is doubtful whether his account of the way they made their cosmic discoveries by chance and intuition as well as by logical thought, really spoils our appreciation of these discoveries. If an understanding of the historical and psychological conditions in which a scientific discovery is made, can in this respect be of value, why should this not also be the case with a work of art?

In his discussion of ethics, Koestler points out that reductionism has tragic results here. He describes five types of reductionist ethical systems:—[38]

(a) *The reduction of ethical values to zero level*, where man is regarded as exclusively determined by his environment. As an example he examines the expression: *tout comprendre, c'est tout pardonner*. In condemning Nazism and the crimes it perpetrated, he argues, one assumes that the individual Nazi has had, within certain limits, a choice of being a Nazi or not. If this is the case, he ought not to be pardoned for actions he freely performed. If, on the other hand, we concentrate merely on the historical, racial and environmental factors underlying the Nazi's behaviour, we might then pardon him by saying that he was not responsible for his actions. But according to Koestler, we only do this by reducing him to an automaton—a creature solely determined by environmental factors, and thereby exclude him from the level on which we make ethical judgments.

But Koestler assumes, at least here, that we only have two clear-cut alternatives, either man is a free agent and therefore responsible for his actions, or his behaviour is strictly determined by his environment. Koestler admits that an individual's freedom is limited, but he does not draw the conclusion that it is limited not only by his personal make-up but also by the social and historical pressures which form the context of his decisions. Because of this, it may not be possible to say that an individual is completely guilty or completely innocent. Koestler implicitly recognizes this in *The Ghost in the Machine*, where he says that our freedom is interfered with by the 'self-assertive, hunger-rage-fear-rape class of emotions' when they are strongly roused. The control of our decisions is then taken over by more primitive levels—'the Beast in us'. This loss of freedom is reflected in the legal concept of diminished responsibility.[39] However, the true position may be that we impute to people responsibilities which are never entirely theirs, and only make allowance for actions which are clearly pathological. This may be seen in the rather arbitrary manner in which legal responsibility has been defined in the past. A person was guilty of a criminal action if he knew that what he was doing was wrong. This sort of definition, however, runs into difficulties if it is possible for a person to know that what he is doing is wrong, without being able to prevent himself from doing it. And the concept of legal responsibility has to be redefined so as to make allowance for what is termed irresistible impulse.[40]

(b) *The application of biological laws to human ethical problems.* This, Koestler says, leads to Darwinistic conceptions such as the notion of the natural rights of the Superman as exhibited in the ethics of Fascism.

(c) *The reduction of ethical values to psychological factors.* One example is the reduction of such social values as courage and self-sacrifice to the psychological level of masochism and the death instinct. Another example is the identification of conscience with the Freudian super-ego—conceived as the introjection of parental authority within oneself. But this, for Koestler, leaves out the essential fact that a good or bad conscience is based on the conviction that the act in question was freely chosen.

Merleau-Ponty has commented on this argument.[41] Koestler, he says, is wrong for not wishing to look more closely into masochism and the death instinct or into childhood conflicts, for an understanding of such human traits as courage and self-sacrifice (especially as Koestler has done something similar in his explanation of political behaviour). He believes they give us a first sketch of the human drama which will later be more clearly expressed through the activities of the adult. By neglecting the psychological and historical context of an individual's life and work, Koestler, Merleau-Ponty goes on, closes the path to psychological analysis and criticism of ourselves and turns us over to the 'mystifications of a good conscience'. But, he says, how can we be sure of the authenticity of the voice of our conscience—that the actions we perform as a result of its promptings, are the right ones? What are our criteria for deciding they are authentic and that we are not being deceived?

(d) *The transfer from the physical to the ethical level of the principle of quantitative measurement.* We cannot, Koestler says, apply arithmetic to the individual's moral choices in terms of such utilitarian formulae as the greatest happiness of the greatest number.

(e) *Yogi ethics,* which endeavour to transfer values derived from passive contemplation into practical action. This, he thinks, leads to the dangers of quietism, escapism and sinning by omission. But Koestler still believes that contemplation remains the only source of guidance in ethical dilemmas. It is however, a little difficult to see why a reliance on values derived by contemplation should necessarily lead to quietism. Quite often it can lead to a very harsh sergeant-major type of morality, as in Kant's dictum that under no circumstances is it justifiable to tell a lie, because one would then be involved in a moral contradiction.

As a basis and guide to aesthetics and ethics, Koestler advocates a 'cosmic hedonism'. By this he means a 'hedonism' which takes account of both the self-assertive and self-transcending impulses. In this way he thinks the individual's social integration may be achieved without his natural appetites being thwarted, thus providing a system of values in which the satisfaction derived from the self-transcending impulses 'makes the pleasure principle morality's guide'.[42] But such pleasure, he notes, is of an entirely different quality from that derived from the self-assertive impulses. Thus he distinguishes between the pleasure he gets in denying himself a drink and the pleasure derived from having one. As another example, he considers the artist and his audience who derive aesthetic pleasure from experiences which under other conditions would be distasteful to them. This may be seen in tragedy, as when an actor plays the harrowing role of King Lear. He may obtain considerable pleasure from playing the role, and so may the members of the audience, despite their occasional wiping away of a tear.

But in introducing different kinds of pleasure, Koestler, like J. S. Mill, seems to imply that one kind of pleasure (i.e., that got from the self-transcending impulses) is better or higher than another. Koestler could argue, however, that these higher kinds of pleasure which he identifies with ethical and aesthetic values, are not introduced from outside the hierarchical system which is our society, as is the case with pure (or Platonic) values, but emerge at a higher level of it. This, no doubt, is why he calls his ethical system a 'natural' one. But if this is the case, then he would seem to assume that it is society itself which gives its approval to the self-transcending impulses. However, Koestler does admit that these impulses will not in themselves necessarily lead to moral action. He points out that 'the crimes of violence committed for selfish, personal motives are historically insignificant compared to those committed *ad majorem gloriam Dei*, out of self-sacrificing devotion to a flag, a leader, a religious faith or a political conviction'.[43] Koestler seems to be saying that the fact that an individual sacrifices himself for a cause, for example, Nazism, does not necessarily mean that his action is praiseworthy, since the cause may not be. One might indeed be inclined to draw a similar conclusion about Rubishov's own behaviour in *Darkness at Noon*. Further, even if the cause is a worthy one, if its pursuit results in dire misery to others, as was the case

35

with the Counter-Reformation and its use of the Inquisition, then this brings the ideals themselves into disrepute.

The Trivial and Tragic Planes

One of the most interesting features of Koestler's work is his doctrine of the trivial and tragic planes. By the trivial plane, he has in mind our everyday existence where we are largely concerned with humdrum events; and by the tragic or cosmic plane, that level of existence in which we find ourselves when faced with some crisis. The average person, he tells us, in an industrialized society, lives practically all his life on the trivial plane, and only comes into contact with the tragic plane on a few occasions, e.g., at puberty, when he falls in love, or in the presence of death.[44] Koestler thinks that the essential point of the so-called existentialist philosophy is just this emphasis on catastrophic crises in which the individual becomes truly free—or integrated in a higher synthesis; in other words, when he exercises his freedom under the stress and strain of extreme circumstances.

In an essay, 'In memory of Richard Hillary', Koestler explores this question in some detail. Hillary was a young Oxford undergraduate who joined the R.A.F. during the last war, became a fighter pilot, was badly burned, and when he returned to active service was killed in an accident during a night training flight. The essay quotes from one of Hillary's letters, in which reference is made to Koestler's theory of the trivial and tragic planes. Hillary points out that one of the miseries of the human condition is that we cannot live permanently on one or other of these planes, but oscillate between them. When we are on the trivial plane, the realities of the other are nonsense—overstrung nerves; when we are on the tragic plane, the joys and sorrows of the other level are shallow and trivial. He goes on, 'if one has to live through a long stretch of time in physical danger, one is placed as it were on the intersection line of the two planes; a curious situation which is a kind of tight-rope walking on one's nerves. As few people can bear it for long, they elaborate conventions and formulae —e.g., R.A.F. slang and understatement. In other words, they try to assimilate the tragic with the trivial plane'.[45]

For Koestler, 'It is this jump from one plane to the other which transforms undergraduates into heroes'.[46] He notes that whereas the pilot can only stand the strain by projecting the tragic on to the trivial plane, the artist, on the other hand, proceeds the opposite way: he tries to see the trivial from the point of view of the tragic plane. Great art, Koestler says, has its origins in the artist's attempt to depict everyday events on such a cosmic plane. This may be seen not only in literature and drama, but also in such visual arts as painting and sculpture.

In both *Insight and Outlook* and *The Act of Creation*, Koestler takes this oscillation between the trivial and tragic planes as a model, not only of artistic creation, but also of scientific discovery and humour. The creative act (which he calls the *Eureka* process, after Archimedes) will only occur, he says, if there is a creative stress, a tension between the two planes of existence: the trivial plane of daily routine and the tragic or cosmic plane, and an urge to unify them on a higher level. In the field of scientific discovery this tension between the two planes is seen in situations where the scientist suddenly discovers the connection between trivial events and a general law of nature. Koestler quotes, among other examples, that of Newton's apochryphal apple and the law of gravitation.

The essence of Koestler's theoretical position regarding the creative act is to be found in his notion of the intersection or 'bisociation' of two such incompatible frameworks of reference. He argues that the higher mental functions as they occur in humour, art and discovery, can only be described in bisociative terms rather than in terms of 'association', where we are largely concerned with the logical connections of ideas within a single system.

In *The Act of Creation*, he gives a more formal account of the creative process. It is '*the perceiving of a situation or idea, L, in two self-consistent but habitually incompatible frames of reference, M_1 and M_2*. The event L, in which the two intersect, is made to vibrate simultaneously on two different wavelengths, as it were. While this unusual situation lasts, L is not merely linked to one associative context, but *bisociated* with two'.[47] Koestler's point is that whereas our routine adaptations are associative, i.e., they move within one framework of reference, original adaptations such as creative achievements in art and scientific thought are bisociative, i.e., they oscillate between two such systems. The concept of bisociation would then seem to be a generalization of his doctrine of the trivial and tragic planes.

It is interesting to note that the approach to human existence in terms of such strong incompatible frameworks, which we need to reconcile by way of a synthesis, has overtones of the Hegelian dialectic with its thesis and antithesis, where progress is made by means of the synthesis of such opposites. In the light of Koestler's hierarchical approach to the organism one wonders, however, whether he has not taken the physical concepts of disequilibrium and equilibrium, and applied them somewhat loosely to the field of creative thought.

The Three Domains of Creativity

For Koestler these three domains of creativity, humour, scientific discovery, and art, shade into each other. Although the logical pattern is the same—the discovery of hidden similarities—the emotional climate is different in each of these three cases. The comic simile, he says, has a touch of aggressiveness, whereas scientific reasoning by analogy is emotionally detached, i.e., neutral. On the other hand, the poetic image may be sympathetic or admiring. All patterns of creative activity are then, according to Koestler, trivalent—i.e., can be manifested in each of three forms, as either humour, discovery or art.

To bring out the fluidity of the boundaries between science and art, Koestler gives a number of examples: the mathematician, he says, talks of elegant solutions; the surgeon, of a beautiful operation; the literary critic, of 'two-dimensional' characters. Science, he continues, is said to aim at truth, art at beauty; but the criteria of truth (such as verifiability) are not as clear-cut as we tend to believe and even less so are the criteria

38

of beauty. Koestler is pointing out that scientific theories, however well they have been authenticated, can at the most only be said to be probable. In mathematics, too, certainty has proved to be an unattainable ideal; the undecidability of certain kinds of statement and the hypothetical character of others have made us revise our views on mathematical certainty. Conversely, Koestler notes that in the field of the visual arts such mathematical notions as the laws of proportion and perspective have been taken by artists as guides to their depiction of nature.

Humour

Koestler starts his account of the creative act with an analysis of humour because, as he tells us, humour is the only field of creative activity where a stimulus on a high level of complexity produces a clearly defined physiological reflex. He distinguishes between the release of emotional tension in tragedy and humour as follows. In tragedy the tension increases until the climax is reached: for example, Othello kills Desdemona; then it slowly ebbs away and produces a cathartic effect. He quotes Aristotle here: 'horror and pity accomplish the purgation of the emotions'.[48] In humour, on the other hand, we get a somewhat different pattern of tension release. Koestler relates the anecdote of the marquis who on returning home finds his wife in the arms of a bishop. The marquis proceeds to the window and goes through the motions of blessing the people. 'What are you doing?' cries his anguished wife. The marquis replied, 'Monseigneur is performing my functions, so I am performing his'. In this anecdote, Koestler states, the tension mounts as the story progresses, but it never reaches its expected climax—the marquis assaulting the bishop. The marquis' unexpected reaction upsets our dramatic expectations. There is, as a result, a sudden relief of tension, and we burst into laughter. Koestler believes that since the aggressive emotions are more primitive, they continue to persist after the reason for their occurrence has ceased. Thus the emotional tension generated by the narrative finds its release in laughter which allows the surplus emotions to run to earth, as it were.

Matrices and Codes

Koestler uses the word 'matrix' in connection with any ability, habit or skill governed by a code of fixed rules. A skill, for example, is under the control (a) of a fixed code of rules (which may be innate or acquired by learning) and (b) of a flexible strategy, guided by environmental pointers. For example, on a lowly animal level, a spider will spin its web according to certain instinctive constraints, which broadly determine the web's characteristic pattern, but the pattern of the web will also depend on the environment in which the spider finds itself. Similarly, in our playing of such games as chess, though we need to keep to the rules of the game, we will vary our strategy in accordance with our opponent's play. Mathematical reasoning is, of course, the case *par excellence* where our performance is governed by specific rules. Verbal reasoning too follows rules, the most obvious being those of grammar and syntax. But semantic codes also come in. For example, Koestler says, we may discuss the problem of capital punishment in terms of social utility or religious morality or psychopathology. He claims that each of these universes of discourse is governed by a set of rules, some operating on conscious and others on unconscious levels, and comprising axiomatic beliefs and prejudices.

According to Koestler, we can escape from our more or less automatized routines of thinking and believing in two ways: (1) through dreaming and dream-like states when rational thought is, as it were, suspended and we regress to more primitive levels of experience; or (2) through a spontaneous flash of insight, which shows a familiar situation or event in a new light in terms of a previously unconnected matrix, so that we ascend to a new more complex mental level. These two processes, he believes, are intimately connected.

As we have seen, Koestler considers the bisociative pattern entering into the creative act to be trivalent: that is, it can produce comic, tragic or intellectually important effects, according to the emotional climate in which it exhibits itself. As an example of this, he considers the schoolboy's prank of partially sawing off the legs of his master's chair, so that when

40

the latter sits on it, it collapses and with it his dignity. For Koestler, this example can be changed from a comic into a tragic or purely intellectual experience by a simple change of emotional climate. Thus, the master's wife would see it as a tragic happening, whereas a medical man would proceed in a matter of fact way to see whether the master had broken any bones. Koestler claims that, although both Bergson's and Freud's theories of humour also try to explain humour in terms of the intersection of incongruous frameworks, they do not throw light on the relatedness of humour with art and scientific discovery.

Scientific Discovery and Invention

For Koestler, intellectual curiosity plays a very important part in science, so that it would be wrong to regard science as having always had a strictly utilitarian function. He sees two sides to the manifestation of emotions at the moment of discovery. There is (1) a triumphant explosion of tension: surplus emotion is suddenly released as a result of the problem being solved. An example of this is Archimedes running out of his bath shouting *Eureka*! In other cases, he tells us, there is (2) the slow fading afterglow—a contemplative delight closely related to an aesthetic appreciation of beauty. Archimedes, he says, may have had this latter experience later on in the day, when he found pleasure in the simple relationship between volume and density. Koestler's description of the emotional dynamics of scientific discovery and their close connection with aesthetic appreciation, is of considerable interest. One wonders, however, whether his explanation of such phenomena in terms of the throwing off of excess emotion, either suddenly in the case of laughter or gradually as in emotional catharsis, is really an explanation at all, since it seems to be little more than a description of the emotional aftermath of problem-solving and aesthetic appreciation.

Koestler notes that discovery is usually taken as seeing an analogy which nobody has seen before. In his view, however, the act of discovery has both a disruptive and constructive aspect. It must first disrupt the habitual patterns of mental

41

organization before a new synthesis can be achieved. He gives an example of this from Kohler's book *The Mentality of Apes*, where a chimpanzee called Sultan, faced with the problem of obtaining a banana which was beyond his reach, breaks off a branch and uses it to drag the banana towards him. Sultan's way of looking at the tree, Koestler says, had to be broken up, and he had to see that the branch could be detached from it and used as an instrument.

At a higher level of intellectual activity, Koestler quotes Archimedes' discovery of the specific gravity of substances. Archimedes' problem was to find out whether King Hiero's crown was made of gold or adulterated with a baser metal. He noticed that the water level rose when he immersed himself in his bath, and thus hit on the fact that the volume of water displaced was equal to the immersed part of his body, whose volume could hence be measured.

After the event, Koestler notes in *Insight and Outlook*, it is easy to make the process appear as one of deductive reasoning and to express it in the form of the following syllogism:—

> The volume of a liquid is easy to measure.
> The volume of a solid is equal to the volume of
> the liquid displaced by its immersion.
> Therefore: The volume of a solid can be
> measured by the volume of the liquid displaced
> by its immersion.[49]

This syllogistic scheme, Koestler says, gives the impression that the mental achievement consists in bringing together the two premises, but it gives no indication of the process of discovery which preceeded it.

Koestler argues that our seeing of analogies is not simply the uncovering of already existing but hidden relationships, but is established by a process of selective emphasis, which brings together hitherto unrelated aspects of things, and that this is dependent on the originality of the scientist's unconscious mind. To illustrate this point, he considers examples from science and technology: Gutenberg's invention of printing with movable type; Kepler's synthesis of astronomy and physics; and Darwin's theory of evolution by natural selection.[50]

42

1. Gutenberg was acquainted with printing by means of engraved wooden blocks (which had been introduced from China). These, when applied to the paper or vellum, had to be rubbed to give an imprint. He tried to find a simpler method, and hit upon the idea of casting letters in metal which could be used like a coin punch on metal or a seal on wax to give an imprint. This was the origin of movable type, since the cast letters could be used in different combinations to form words. But such letters can never make a clear imprint by the rubbing method. At a wine harvest, Gutenberg noticed the wine press which exerts considerable pressure on the grapes, thus extracting the juice. He then, as Koestler says, bisociated the wine press and the seal, which added together gave the letter press with its clearer imprint.

2. Before Kepler, the orbits of the planets were described in purely geometrical terms, in terms of epicycles which were circles geared as it were to other circles. It was thought that, since the heavens were perfect, the planetary orbits had to be described in terms of perfect or circular motions. But as the observed orbits of the planets appeared otherwise, the only way 'to save the appearances' was by the use of such epicycles. As a result of his observations and calculations, Kepler became convinced that the orbits were elliptical. Up to then, it had been thought that physics applied only to terrestrial objects and not to heavenly ones. Now Kepler, as it were, jettisoned the geometrical framework and tried to see the orbits of the planets in terms of a physical framework. And so he explained the elliptic orbits by saying that there were antagonistic forces acting on the planets: one located in the planet, the other in the sun. These formed, as it were, the two foci of the ellipse. In this way Kepler combined (or bisociated) astronomy previously thought to be a purely geometrical science with physics previously thought to be a terrestrial one.

3. Darwin accepted the evolutionary view current at his time, that the various organic species had not been independently created, but had descended from other species. He also knew that domestic breeds of animals could be improved by *artificial* selection, i.e., the selective mating of favourable variations. On reading Malthus' *An Essay on the Principle of*

Population, he noted Malthus' idea that any species which had features profitable to it in the struggle for existence against other species tended to survive—they were *naturally* selected. Malthus' population theory which explains why one species multiplies at the cost of others, was according to Koestler married by Darwin to the earlier evolutionary theory. Darwin thus made the struggle for existence (*natural* selection) the causative mechanism of evolutionary improvement.

It might, of course, be said that Koestler has selected cases which fit neatly into his bisociative model, and that there are other cases of scientific discovery which do not fit in so easily. In the field of microphysics, for example, it is difficult to see how quantum theory could be a synthesis of more familiar macroscopic systems. And to say, as Koestler does, that such a process of selective emphasis depends on the originality of the scientist's unconscious mind, is not to say anything very illuminating: if the statement is intended as an explanation of the creative act, then it would seem to be circular.

Chance and Ripeness

Koestler points out that Archimedes' mental skill in manipulating abstract concepts like volume and density made him ripe for his discovery. He believes that the more ripe a situation is for the discovery of a new synthesis, the less need there is for chance to enter in. So he draws the reader's attention to the phenomenon of multiple discoveries—that certain scientific discoveries have been made simultaneously by different people. For example, Newton and Leibniz co-discovered the calculus, and Darwin and Wallace formulated the theory of evolution at about the same time. Koestler is not at all concerned with whether, if Newton and Leibniz had not lived, someone else would have discovered the calculus; but rather with how they did it. He does not believe that chance and ripeness are in themselves adequate as explanatory notions. The notion of the creative individual also has a role to play. Einstein, he tells us, discovered the principle of relativity although the observations on which it is based had been available for at least forty years.

For Koestler, unconscious processes play their part in

scientific discovery. He refers especially to the account given by the famous French mathematician Poincaré of the part played by such activities in his own mathematical discoveries. The solution of one problem came to him after he had drunk black coffee and passed a sleepless night. In another example, Koestler refers us to Kekulé (who was Professor of Chemistry at Ghent) and the dream which he had in 1865 during his afternoon nap in front of the fire. In the course of it, he saw strings of dancing atoms transforming themselves into serpents and swallowing their tails. This dream observation formed the basis of his radical proposal that the molecules of certain organic compounds are not open structures but closed rings, of which the Benzene ring is a good example.

Koestler believes that, in the process of scientific discovery, logic and intuition form the two extremes of a continuous scale. At one end, we have discoveries which seem to be due to more or less step by step conscious logical reasoning, and, at the other, to spontaneous intuitive insights. He claims that if one looks at the more personal writings of mathematicians and physicists (their letters and autobiographies) one finds an emphasis on creative imagination at the expense of logic: proof and verification only seem to come after the discovery has been made. Koestler sees an apparent paradox here: between the rationality and objectivity of mathematics and physics, on the one hand, and the subjective and irrational mental processes which enter into their construction, on the other.

The classical reply to this sort of approach is to distinguish as Popper does,[51] between the context of discovery and the context of justification. On such a view it would be said that Koestler is largely concerned with the context of discovery— with the psychological processes entering into the construction of a scientific theory. On the other hand, the context of justification is concerned with the testability, logical dependency or contradictory character of the statements making up a scientific theory. Koestler would no doubt reply that the context of justification is merely concerned with a *post factum* analysis of the theory which is itself dependent on the earlier, more intuitive, process of discovery.

The Unconscious

One can see the influence of Freud and Jung[52] in Koestler's analysis of the part played by unconscious processes in scientific discoveries and artistic creation. This is in keeping with the important role Koestler assigns to unconscious processes in the determination of political behaviour, which for long was taken by political theorists to be a purely rational enterprise. Most contemporary philosophical theories still, however, pay little attention to such processes. Koestler is critical of the tradition initiated by Descartes, that all experience is conscious and reflective in character. This view, he says, overestimates the role of strictly rational thought. Not only are the higher levels of thought as exhibited in science and art rooted in the unconscious, but so too are our more trivial thought activities: a point already made by Freud in his account of the psychopathology of everyday life.

On the level of our acquisition of skills, too, the greater our mastery of particular skills, the more automatized and unconscious do they become. When we learn to drive a motor car, we are at first very conscious of such operations as gearchanging, accelerating and braking. With increasing proficiency our awareness of these activities sinks into the unconscious. Only when we are confronted with some unforeseen hazard, do we again turn our attention to our handling of the car's controls. Some skills can become highly automatic, such as that of a bar pianist who can rattle off a tune on the piano without thinking about it. But Koestler goes on to point out that the intervention of unconscious processes in the creative act involves the reverse process: it is a burgeoning forth of ideas from the depths of the unconscious into conscious experience.

In order to clarify the role played by the unconscious in scientific discovery, Koestler takes as his model poetic creation, and as a particular example, Coleridge's 'Kubla Khan'. This was written under the influence of opium, during which Coleridge's thinking was largely in pictorial images. Koestler regards pictorial thinking as a more primitive form of mental activity than conceptual thinking. By thus falling back on the use of visual imagery the poet, he says, regresses to older, more primitive forms of mental activity, as is the case when we dream. The difference, however, between the poet and the dreamer is that the former can alternate between two levels. He can think both in images and verbal concepts at the same time or alternate between them. The scientific counterpart of the Coleridge ('Kubla Khan') episode, Koestler tells us, is Kekulé's dream of the moving serpent swallowing his tail, in which there is a switch from conceptual thought to semi-conscious images.

Koestler thinks that, although language helps us to articulate and make precise our hazy thoughts and vague intuitions, the scientist may be put at a disadvantage by the precision and hidden assumptions embedded in his terminology. This leads to difficulties when developments in science occur, as the logic implicit in these concepts no longer applies to the new theoretical situations. This happened to the Newtonian concepts of space and time with the advent of the theory of relativity, where space and time are no longer regarded as independent. However, even though one may discount the attempt by linguistic philosophers to identify thought and language, one must not overlook the fact that civilization would not have advanced very far without written language, in terms of which the concepts used in both common sense and science can be clearly articulated.

This, of course, does not detract from Koestler's point that the creative act among original thinkers depends upon the working of the unconscious mind, and that this involves a regression to more primitive modes of mental activity as in the dream, where one regresses from the verbal symbol to the pictorial image. For example, Koestler tells us that Einstein sometimes relied on sensations of muscular movement (kinaesthetic sensations) in his thinking. Koestler continues to make the point that the logic of the dream derives from the kind of causation found in primitive societies and the fantasies of childhood. However, it is a little difficult to see how it can be called a logic, since the basic logical laws of identity and contradiction are often breached. Piaget, in his account of language and thought in the child, has shown how the young child is at first oblivious of contradiction, and how his causal explanations are animistic in character.

47

In his discussion of the history of scientific thought, Koestler agrees with the views of T. S. Kuhn expressed in the latter's *The Structure of Scientific Revolutions*,[53] where the distinction is made between paradigm changes in science, i.e., revolutionary crises, and normal or routine science in which these changes are consolidated. What happens, according to Koestler, is that the scientific revolution is turned into an orthodoxy and becomes a closed system of thought which may stand in the way of further advance. In the course of time, he tells us, a new crisis may arise leading to a new synthesis, and the cycle starts again. Koestler, therefore, believes with Kuhn that science advances in a discontinuous, unpredictable way, and exhibits rapid changes of tempo. Koestler also sees an analogy here with the history of art, where, in between periodic upheavals, there are long periods during which the artistic innovation is assimilated.

3

SIGNIFICANCE

IN THE TWENTY or more books he has written, Koestler has covered a wide range of topics: Communism, Zionism, capital punishment, the history of astronomy, psychology, Yoga, Zen Buddhism, modern quantum physics and extra-sensory perception. He is now a naturalized British subject and was recently awarded the honour of Companion of the British Empire.

Philip Toynbee has succinctly described Koestler's intellectual development as follows: Koestler has moved steadily yogi-wards on that scale which he himself invented. At one time he was a member of the Communist Party, a dialectical materialist and something of a behaviourist. He then became for several years our leading anti-Communist intellectual. After campaigning against capital punishment, he began to make himself a leading synthesizer of the two cultures: an opponent of behaviourism and an expounder of all that is most mysterious and least explained both in the sciences and the arts.[54]

Koestler's move to the ultra-violet end of the spectrum seems increasingly to be reflected in the social attitudes of the younger generation. It is doubtful whether Koestler would be over-sympathetic to present-day hippy culture and the espousal by some of its exponents of Buddhism and Yoga. It is also doubtful whether Koestler is essentially a Yogi figure despite his emphasis on our need to develop the art of contemplation. Christmas Humphreys, a prominent English practitioner of Zen Buddhism, once accused Koestler of being too much of a rationalist to appreciate Zen. In reply, Koestler stated that the simple abdication of reason in favour of a spurious mysticism did not resolve the dilemma facing us today between Western rationalism on the one hand, and the Cloud of Unknowning on the other. It is noteworthy that his interest in extra-sensory phenomena does not make him neglect the need for a rational explanation of this phenomenon.

The occasional slighting remarks Koestler makes about philosophers, especially continental ones, constitutes one of the more curious aspects of his work. Despite his evident attraction to British empiricism, because of its championing of tolerance, liberalism and democracy, his overall approach to philosophical problems is more in the continental tradition of Hegel, Marx and Kierkegaard (the Danish philosopher who was the father of modern existentialism). And, as has been pointed out, the influence of Koestler's Marxist past may still be discovered in his work: in the dialectical mode of arguing and in the tendency to express himself in terms of sharply defined opposites. Further, his emphasis on scientific revolutions exhibits overtones of the dialectical conception of history. Although Koestler's style of writing is clear and precise, his method of expressing himself through vivid metaphors and sharp antitheses does sometimes give his descriptions of events and ideas a contrived character.

It is interesting to see that the political extremes, of which the Yogi and the Commissar are examples, are paralleled for Koestler by the cultural extremes of the artist and the scientist. In his attempt to bridge the gap between the arts and the sciences, Koestler has tried to show that psychological factors, sometimes of an irrational sort, enter into the process of scientific discovery as well as into that of artistic creation. Koestler's account of creativity then stresses the more irrational, even mystical, aspects of our experience and the workings of the unconscious mind. Hence, he also sees no conflict between the religious and scientific attitudes.

Koestler does not therefore believe in the neutrality of science, and he regards scientific attempts at explanations of ultimate reality as just as much in the nature of anthropomorphic projections as religion has been. He has been criticized for being an amateur in science, but nevertheless he has the happy knack of being able to explain scientific ideas in simple terms. Bacon, it has been said, wrote of science like a Lord

Chancellor; Koestler, one might claim without disrespect, does so like a novelist. In popular writing in the history of science there are few who can surpass him. His *Sleepwalkers*, for example, is at once enthralling and educative. His scientific writing, however, seems to suffer from a defect similar to that in his political writing, namely a tendency to dramatize and sharpen differences and conflicts by the use of striking metaphors and analogies. At the same time, he often seems to read a greater significance into the similarities he discerns between things and processes than they merit.

An advantage of Koestler's amateur scientific status is that he shows a lack of conventional scientific biases, and with it a tendency to champion what might appear to be scientific lost causes. Thus his interest in neo-Lamarckianism may not be entirely acceptable to the orthodox scientist, nor for that matter may be his interest in extra-sensory perception. But whatever the current scientific view on these questions, it would be foolish to dismiss out of hand such apparent lost causes without closer investigation; and this seems to be the point Koestler is making in such works as *The Case of the Midwife Toad* and *The Roots of Coincidence*.

Koestler comes out strongly against the reductionist and behaviourist accounts of human nature, and because of this he finds himself criticized by those who believe in the sanctity of the scientific method, and who assume that it can be applied to every aspect of human experience. Koestler's work is a valuable corrective to this sort of approach, indicating as it does that, as far as the nature of creativity is concerned, perhaps the only way we can study it at the moment is through the case histories of great scientists and artists.

Koestler therefore believes that the motive forces in scientific development are not only intellectual, but that our emotive attitudes towards the world also play their part. The tension between these two aspects of our experience—the intellectual and the emotive—is clearly seen in his writings, and is at the root of the polar opposites one finds exemplified in the titles of such books as *The Yogi and the Commissar*. This tension in Koestler's thought goes back to his student days. He tells us, 'As a student my interests were about equally divided between engineering and social engineering on the one hand, and the

51

expanding universe of Freud, Jung, Eddington and Jeans, with its irrational and mystic undercurrents on the other. This tug-of-war continued in later life'.[55]

Essentially, Koestler seems to be a rationalist with marked liberal views. His prognostications as to the future of the human race may at times be pessimistic, but they are never without some gleam of hope. His basic outlook on man has been an optimistic, even Utopian, one; and this no doubt explains his disappointment with the outcome of revolutionary movements: he expected too much. Orwell notes this when he says of Koestler that as an ultimate objective he believes in the Earthly Paradise or Utopia, the Sun State which the gladiators set out to establish, but which seems to be receding into the far distance. Koestler, he continues, has described himself as a short-term pessimist. He recognizes the horrors facing the world today, but believes that somehow in the end it will come out all right. But, Orwell goes on, since 1930 the world has given no such reason for optimism. He is himself of the opinion that, 'Men can only be happy when they do not assume that the object of life is happiness'.[56] He does not believe that Koestler will accept this proposition, since he still thinks that the Earthly Paradise is desirable. Perhaps, Orwell continues, whether desirable or not, it is not possible.

Orwell wrote this in 1944, but Koestler's optimism (or short-termed pessimism) is still apparent, though it does now seem to be wearing a little thin. In his essay, 'The Trail of the Dinosaur' (1955), Koestler wrote: 'Once we hoped for Utopia, now, in a chastened mood, we can at best hope for a reprieve; pray for time and play for time'.[57] Short-term measures may gain mankind some time, and this at least gives Koestler a tenuous hope in the possibility of some unexpected mutation in men's dominating passions and interests. The present pressures on humanity may, he says, perhaps be a biological stimulus which will release a new spiritual awareness. Within the not too distant future, he continues, *homo sapiens* will go the way of the dinosaur or mutate towards a stabler future. 'We shall either destroy ourselves or take off to the stars'.[58] To this Orwell might have pessimistically replied: we may do both.

NOTES

1. *The Yogi and the Commissar* (Danube edition), p. 177
2. George Orwell: 'Arthur Koestler', *Critical Essays*, Secker and Warburg, London 1960, p. 162
3. *Darkness at Noon*, dedication
4. *Cf.* Orwell, *Critical Essays*, p. 155
5. David Caute: *Communism and the French Intellectuals*, André Deutsch Ltd. 1964, p. 128
6. *Cf.* John Atkin: *Arthur Koestler*, Neville Spearman, London 1956, p. 180
7. Maurice Merleau-Ponty: *Humanisme et Terreur: Essai sur le problème Communiste*, Gallimard, Paris, 1947
   Maurice Merleau-Ponty (1907–1961) was a co-founder with Jean-Paul Sartre and Simone de Beauvoir of the French Left-wing journal *Les Temps Modernes*. He was professor of philosophy at the Collège de France, and author of *The Phenomenology of Perception* and other works.
8. *Cf.* 'Les dilemmes de Koestler', *Humanisme et Terreur*, pp. 3-26
9. *Ibid.*, p. 19; *Darkness at Noon*, p. 24
10. *The Yogi and the Commissar*, p. 173
11. *Ibid.*, p. 173
12. *Humanisme et Terreur*, p. 161
13. See Atkin's discussion in his chapter, 'The Test of Terror', *Arthur Koestler*, pp. 194–203
14. *Drinkers of Infinity*, p. 281
15. *Ibid.*, p. 285
16. *The Yogi and the Commissar*, p. 15
17. *Ibid.*, pp. 24-5
18. *Cf. Humanisme et Terreur*, p. 181
19. *Cf. Ibid.*, p. 177
20. *Cf. Insight and Outlook*, p. 173
21. Sigmund Freud (1856–1939): founder of the Vienna school of psychoanalysis. Freud drew attention to the importance of the unconscious mind, described its mechanisms and showed that repression of our instinctive drives, particularly sex, led to neurosis. By means of psychoanalytical treatment the patient was made aware of the causes of his neurosis and in this way a cure was achieved.

22. *Cf. The God that Failed* (ed. R. H. S. Crossman) pp. 25-6
23. 'Guide to Political Neuroses', *The Trail of the Dinosaur* (Danube ed.), p. 128
24. *Ibid.*, p. 129
25. *Ibid.*, p. 129
26. *Ibid.*, p. 129
27. *Ibid.*, pp. 130-7
28. *Ibid.*, pp. 137-41
29. *Ibid.*, p. 141
30. *Cf.* Atkin, *Arthur Koestler*, p. 58
31. *Cf. The Act of Creation*, pp. 285-6
32. Koestler in fact refers to James' book as still being the classic in this field. See *The Ghost in the Machine*, p. 260n*
33. *Cf. Insight and Outlook*, pp. 204-20
34. *Cf.* 'The Concept of Hierarchy', *The Act of Creation*, pp. 287-91. Koestler schematically illustrates a hierarchy in *The Act of Creation*, p. 433, as follows:

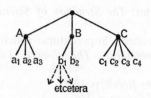

35. *Cf. Insight and Outlook*, pp. 131-4, pp. 214-6
36. *Cf. The Yogi and the Commissar*, p. 223
37. *Ibid.*, p. 224
38. *Cf. Ibid.*, pp. 224-30
39. *Cf. The Ghost in the Machine*, p. 217
40. That Koestler is unhappy about the question of diminished responsibility may be seen from his statement, 'The safest hypothesis is to assign a minimum of responsibility to the other, and a maximum to oneself'. *Ibid.*, p. 218
41. *Cf. Humanisme et Terreur*, p. 178
42. *Insight and Outlook*, p. 228

43. *The Ghost in the Machine*, p. 234. 'The crimes of a Caligula shrink to insignificance compared to the havoc wrought by Torquemada'. *Ibid.*, p. 234
44. *Cf. Insight and Outlook*, p. 378
45. *The Yogi and the Commissar*, p. 64
46. *Ibid.*, p. 65
47. *The Act of Creation*, p. 35
48. *Ibid.*, p. 33
49. *Cf. Insight and Outlook*, p. 254
50. *Cf. The Act of Creation*, pp. 121-44
51. *Cf.* Karl R. Popper: *The Logic of Scientific Discovery*, Hutchinson, London 1959, p. 31
52. Carl Gustuv Jung (1875–1961): Swiss psychiatrist, at one time a disciple of Freud, but broke away to found his own school of analytical psychology. He rejected Freud's theory of the sexual origins of neurosis and emphasized the importance from the point of view of neurosis of inherited dispositions (or archetypes) located in the collective unconscious.
53. Thomas S. Kuhn: *The Structure of Scientific Revolutions*, Chicago, 1962
54. *Cf.* Philip Toynbee: 'Supernatural solicitings': review of *The Roots of Coincidence*. *The Observer*, London, February 6, 1972, p. 31
55. *The Lotus and the Robot*, p. 12
56. Orwell, *Critical Essays*, p. 161
57. *The Trail of the Dinosaur*, pp. 160-1
58. *Ibid.*, p. 160

SHORT READING LIST

The following works deal mainly with Koestler's novels and political writings:

John Atkin: *Arthur Koestler*, Neville Spearman, London 1956. (Concentrates mainly on Koestler as a political writer), Jenni Calder: *Chronicles of Conscience: A Study of George Orwell and Arthur Koestler*, Secker and Warburg, London 1968. (Comparison of Orwell and Koestler as writers with a social purpose).

A list of Koestler's works is given below.

Novels

> *The Gladiators*, Jonathan Cape, London 1939, Macmillan, NY, 1967
>
> *Darkness at Noon*, Jonathan Cape, London 1940, Macmillan, NY, 1971, Paper, Bantam, 1970
>
> *Arrival and Departure*, Jonathan Cape, London 1943, Macmillan, NY, 1967
>
> *Thieves in the Night*, Macmillan, London 1949, Macmillan, NY, 1967
>
> *The Age of Longing*, William Collins, London 1951, Macmillan, NY, 1954
>
> *The Call Girls*, Hutchinson, London, 1972

Autobiography

> *Spanish Testament*, Victor Gollancz, London 1937
>
> *Dialogue with Death*, Jonathan Cape, London 1940, Macmillan, NY, 1960
>
> *Scum of the Earth*, Jonathan Cape, London 1941, Macmillan, NY, 1968
>
> *The God that Failed* (edited by Richard Crossman), Hamish Hamilton, London 1950, Harper & Row, NY, 1950
>
> *Arrow in the Blue*, Collins and Hamish Hamilton, London 1952, Macmillan, NY, 1970
>
> *The Invisible Writing*, Collins and Hamish Hamilton, London 1954, Macmillan, NY, 1970

Essays: Political and Social

> *The Yogi and the Commissar*, Jonathan Cape, London 1945, Macmillan, NY, 1967

Promise and Fulfilment, Macmillan, London 1949, Macmillan, NY, 1954

The Trail of the Dinosaur, William Collins, London 1955, Macmillan, NY, 1955

Reflections on Hanging, Victor Gollancz, London 1956, Macmillan, NY, 1958

The Lotus and the Robot, Hutchinson, London 1960, Harper & Row, NY, 1961

The Suicide of a Nation (by Fairlie and others), Hutchinson, London 1963, Macmillan, NY, 1969

Drinkers of Infinity, Hutchinson, London 1968, Macmillan, NY, 1969

Books on Creativity and Science

Insight and Outlook, Macmillan, London 1949, U. of Nebraska Press, 1965

The Sleepwalkers, Hutchinson, London 1959, Macmillan, NY, 1968, Paper, Grossett & Dunlap, NY, 1963

The Act of Creation, Hutchinson, London 1964, Macmillan, NY, 1969 & 1970, Paper, Dell, 1966

The Ghost in the Machine, Hutchinson, London 1967, Macmillan, NY, 1968, Paper, Regnery

Beyond Reductionism (edited with J. R. Smythies), Hutchinson, London 1969, Macmillan, NY, 1970, Paper, Beacon, Boston, 1969

The Case of the Midwife Toad, Hutchinson, London 1971, Random House, NY, 1972

The Roots of Coincidence, Hutchinson, London 1972

Theatre
Twilight Bar, Jonathan Cape, London 1945

The above bibliography gives the first date of publication of each book, but some of them have been reissued by other publishers at later dates. A star against a book indicates that it has been republished in the *Danube Edition* by Hutchinson. In cases where Koestler's works have been published in the U.S.A., the name of the American publisher is given after each reference.